DK Machines at work
FIRE TRUCK

LONDON, NEW YORK,
MUNICH, MELBOURNE, and DELHI

Written and edited by Caroline Bingham
Designed by Jacqueline Gooden

Managing editor Susan Leonard
Managing art editor Clare Shedden
US editor Christine Heilman
Jacket design Dean Price
Picture researcher Bridget Tilly
Production Linda Dare
DTP Designer Almudena Díaz
Consultant Martin Cross (UK)
and Fire Chief Steve Hinch (US)

First American edition, 2003
03 04 05 06 07 10 9 8 7 6 5 4 3 2 1
Published in the United States by
DK Publishing, Inc.
375 Hudson Street
New York, New York 10014

Copyright © 2003 Dorling Kindersley Limited

Library of Congress Cataloging-in-Publication Data

Bingham, Caroline, 1962-
Fire truck / Caroline Bingham.-- 1st American ed.
p. cm. -- (Machines at work)
Includes index.
Summary: Introduces fire trucks and the work that they help
firefighters do in all kinds of settings.
ISBN 0-7894-9221-0
1. Fire trucks--Juvenile literature. [1. Fire engines. 2. Fire
extinction.] I. Title. II. Series: Machines at work
(DK Publishing,Inc.)
TH9372 .B55 2003
628.9'25--dc21
2002014865

Color reproduction by GRB Editrice, S.r.l., Verona, Italy
Printed and bound in China by Toppan Printing Co., Ltd.

see our complete
product line at
www.dk.com

Contents

Let's fight fire

When an emergency call reaches the fire station the **firefighters** spring into action. Poles are a fast way down. Then they jump into the waiting fire truck and pull on their **uniforms**.

Ready for a quick change

The firefighters' protective uniforms are always left ready to pull on, with the pants over the boots. It means they can get dressed in seconds.

First the firefighter climbs into the boots.

Next he pulls up the thick, fire-resistant pants.

He is dressed and ready to go in just 30 seconds!

Fire! Fire!

On their way

Once all of the firefighters are aboard, they drive to the fire as fast as they can. That's when you hear the truck's loud siren.

Turntable ladder fire truck

It's a fact

In a major city, a fire station may respond to more than 7,000 calls a year.

Between 4 and 10 firefighters can sit in a fire truck's cab, depending on its size.

T-1

Reflective strips will show up in thick smoke.

Down to work

At the site of a fire, the firefighters begin to unload and connect **hoses**. Some hoses pick up **water** from hydrants. Others are used to spray water over the fire.

Hydrants act like faucets to the main water supply. In some countries they can be seen on the streets.

Keep on pumping

A fire engine acts as a pump, pushing water through hoses to the firefighters. The fire engine pumps the water so powerfully that two or three firefighters may be needed to control just one hose.

Old methods

The earliest firefighting tool was a bucket. It was not a good way to fight fire. This leather and wood bucket was used over 300 years ago.

Many fire engines carry more than 1,600 feet (480 meters) of hose.

PARAMEDIC ENGINE

CASTLE ROCK FIRE/RESCUE

CRFD

ROCK

At the scene

All sorts of machines are called out to a fire, from fire **trucks** to **ambulances**. Sometimes you may spot a fire **chief's** car.

Oxygen bottle   Mask

Circular saw

Jaws of Life®

We have the power!

Some of the firefighter's tools are power-assisted. Here, a huge saw helps a firefighter to get into a building, while the Jaws of Life® are used to pry open a car.

Hydraulic platform fire truck

Around the world, the fire chief takes charge of the crews at a fire.

Fire chief's car

An open house

A fire station is on call 24 hours a day. This means that there's always a team of firefighters ready to respond to an emergency call.

Water power

The most important firefighter's weapon is water, and the fire trucks may have to pump huge amounts of water to put out a fire.

Up the ladder

Fire trucks that carry telescopic ladders are used to observe and fight fires from above and to rescue people.

A hose runs up the ladder to the platform.

Nozzle attack
The nozzle at the top of the ladder lets the firefighters fight a fire from above. They can control the water flow from the ground.

Step onto the platform...
Some fire trucks have a platform at the top of the ladder. People can step onto this from a building and step off at ground level.

The platform can be raised to the height of a 7-story building.

...or use a ladder
A turntable ladder extends up a long way. This one will rise 105 feet (32 meters). The bottom rests on a turntable that can turn the ladder in a full circle.

NEW ROCHELLE

NEW ROCHELLE

LADDER 1
Co. 13

105 FT

NEW ROCHELLE 13

serving Since 1889

ABERDEEN FIRE DEPT.

TRUCK 231

Water works

The most familiar fire engine is a **pumper**. Pumpers carry huge water **tanks** and hundreds of yards of hose. Most importantly they have a powerful **pump**.

All pumped out

Pumpers are usually the first to reach a fire, and their crew will quickly find the nearest water supply. This might be a hydrant, or a pond, stream, or river.

A never-ending task

Following a fire, each hose has to be rolled up. The hoses are made of rubber-lined plastic so they don't rot.

Water intake valve

Where do you need it?

In rural areas there may be no hydrant. The firefighters deal with this by setting up a portable tank. This will be filled with hundreds of gallons of water from water tanker trucks.

A pumper pulls, or drafts, water out of the portable tank and sends it on to the firefighters.

The tanker fills the portable tank in about three minutes.

Pumpers have to carry at least 44 feet (13.5 meters) of ladders.

ENGINE 1231

Equipment is stored in lockers.

Water intake valve.

Rescue units often have a control room inside.

To the rescue

Rescue units carry more tools and equipment than other fire engines. They are called out for all sorts of reasons—and not just for fires.

The power of air

This rescue vehicle is being used in a training exercise with a mock traffic accident. The firefighters are using an airbag to lift the car.

An air line runs from the rescue vehicle to a control valve.

The firefighter controls air flow to the two airbags. Each has its own air line.

Air line

Control room

WYCKOFF FIRE DEPT. RESCUE

Oxygen tanks   Chainsaw   Wooden blocks

What's inside?

A rescue vehicle carries everything you can think of and more—from saws and goggles to resuscitators and airbags.

Sliding panels provide easy access to tools.

Airbag

Wooden blocks are used to support the car as it rises.

Wooden block

At the airport

Large **airports** have their own fire stations. An airport crash truck is very **powerful**, and carries more water and foam than an ordinary fire truck.

Airport firefighters wear fireproof silver suits.

Water control

As well as using hoses, the firefighters can direct streams of foam onto a fire from the two monitors on the cab. These are controlled from inside the cab.

 Monitor

This airport crash truck carries six times more water than a street fire truck.

Monitor

Heavy-duty fire attack

Airport crash trucks are so heavy that they need huge wheels to support them—but they can still reach 50 mph (80 km/h) in 35 seconds!

Air attack

When fire breaks out in a **forest**, the best way to fight it is from above. A firefighting **plane** will drench the fire with water again and again.

Down for a pickup...
The plane swoops down to fill its tanks from the surface of a lake, a river, or the sea.

...and off
The plane takes just 12 seconds to complete its sweep across the surface of the water. Its tanks are now full.

At top speed the plane travels more than three times as fast as a car on a highway.

Before the water is dropped, it is mixed with foam to help smother the flames.

Firefighting
A firefighting plane can get to a fire safely from above, and normally reaches a fire much faster than a ground crew. This is important because a forest fire spreads incredibly fast.

19

Monster attack

Huge firefighting planes called **airtankers** are used to drop thousands of gallons of fire retardant on **forest fires**. This helps to slow down the fire.

Back at base
The retardant is a red liquid that slows down and cools a fire. It is mixed up on the ground before being pumped into the air tanker. Workers handling it have to wear breathing equipment.

Why is it red?
The retardant contains a red dye to make it show up, so that the firefighters know where it has fallen. It soon fades.

Huge doors open
to release the
retardant.

This plane can carry
and drop 3,000
gallons (11,300
liters) of retardant.

Danger flight
The pilot has to fly in very
dangerous conditions, while keeping
to the flight line. After a drop the
plane will head back to base to refill
its tanks. This might take an hour.

It's a fact

There are
different types of
airtanker. All of them
are converted from
old military planes.

The chopper crew

Helicopters are useful firefighting weapons, especially for fires that break out in remote, wooded areas.

On its way...

A helicopter may first ferry ground firefighters to a spot near the fire. It will then collect water from a nearby lake or river and return within minutes.

The bucket can be used to pick up water from very shallow lakes.

...and down it goes

A helicopter will hover close to a fire before dropping its water load. More than 265 gallons (1,000 liters) of water floods down onto a fire's hot spot.

A mighty thirst

This helicopter, known as a Helitanker, sucks up water through a hose called a snorkel. It sucks quickly, filling its 2,500-gallon (9,500-liter) tank in just 45 seconds. It can drop the load in just three seconds.

The snorkel acts just like a big straw.

It's a fact

🚒 A helicopter may make up to 14 drops each hour, depending on how far it is to the nearest water.

🚒 The Helitanker's water can be dropped as a mist or in a torrent.

On the water

If a fire breaks out on a ship, or in a harbor-side building, **fireboats** and **tugs** are used to help put it out. They have an unlimited supply of water!

If the ship doesn't sink, the remains will be towed back to port and either repaired or broken up.

Use that tug

Large harbors use sturdy tugs to help guide ships and barges in and out of port, or tow broken-down boats to a mooring. Tugs are also valuable firefighting machines.

It's a fact

🚒 Tugs look small, but they are powerful—the engines have the power of about 25 trucks.

🚒 Tugs can move ships that are thousands of times their own weight.

🚒 With all monitors working, a fireboat can pump about five times the water of a fire engine.

Let's celebrate!
Fireboats can also be used to celebrate events. Shooting their water cannons, or monitors, at full power, they look very impressive.

In control
Fireboats have a number of monitors. These can be operated from the bridge or by hand.

Water jets can reach 295 feet (90 meters).

Foam is mixed with the water to fight oil-based fires.

Training day

Safety, fire behavior, dangerous fumes...firefighters have a lot to learn. In many countries they do this at special training **schools**.

Fire it up!
Instructors use computers to control the fires at this US training school. They can control the spread and the height, and even put out a fire if necessary.

Extinguisher action
This replica steel car is used to teach firefighters how to deal with a car on fire. An extinguisher is used to spray a chemical powder, starving the fire of oxygen.

The smoke looks bad, but these fires release no dangerous fumes.

Dressed in silver
Here the firefighters are directing a high-pressure hose on a mock aircraft fire. Airport firefighters have to wear fireproof silver suits.

What's a flashover?

A flashover happens when a fire has been burning for some time. The air gets so hot that everything in the room bursts into flames. If it does happen, the firefighters have two seconds to escape.

The firefighters learn to cool the ceiling before they attack the fire.

Can it be stopped?

Flashovers can be fought by directing water at the ceiling to cool it down. If a trainee firefighter forgets to do this, the instructor can create a mock flashover.

Days of old

The **sleek** firefighting machines and the equipment of today are very different from the firefighting **machines** of old. The main difference is in the **power**.

Horse drawn
Steam pumpers were drawn by teams of horses. The horses were trained to respond to the station's bell.

Hands to the pump
In the 1700s fire engines pumped by hand came into use. This two-person pump would have delivered the power to pump a garden hose.

Each handle was pulled down in turn.

Hand-powered pump

Steam pumper fire engine

Steam chimney

All steamed up
Steam power provided more water flow from the hoses. This pump dates from 1901.

Put it out!
Fire extinguishers have been used for many years. In the mid-1800s one method used the reaction of soda and acid to force water out.

Soda-acid extinguisher

Hand-pump extinguisher

Muffin bell

Sound alert
Hand-held bells were once used to warn people of a fire.

Fire engines always carry alarm bells or sirens.

Early 20th century TT Ford fire engine

Motor power
With the invention of the car, fire engines speeded up. The extra power also allowed them to carry more equipment.

Picture gallery

Firefighting airplane

The number of drops a scooping airplane can make depends on the distance to a suitable water source.

Rescue unit

There are different kinds of rescue units, depending on what kind of rescue is needed in the local area.

Fireboat

This fireboat's engines are ten times as powerful as those on a fire engine.

Hydraulic platform

The highest hydraulic platform currently available can reach the 33rd story.

Turntable ladder

Water can be sprayed from the ladder hose at the rate of 1,000 gallons a minute.

Pumper

Pumpers are usually the first fire engines to leave the station.

Fire chief's car

A fire chief's car may be used for visits to local schools or businesses.

Firefighting helicopter

This helicopter can pick up water from a water source that is just 18 inches (45 cm) deep.

Old fire engine

Firefighters clung on to the sides of early fire engines, standing on steps called running boards.

Airport crash truck

This fire truck carries a heat-seeking camera on top of the cab. It pinpoints hot spots inside a burning airplane.

Glossary

Airbag a bag that can be blown up to raise and support a vehicle.

Breathing apparatus the oxygen bottle and mask that a firefighter uses to breathe when there is smoke.

Control room an area inside a rescue unit that can be used by the fire chief.

Flashover this happens when the heat of a fire sets fire to all the items in a room.

Hydrant this is like a huge faucet to the main underground water system. Hydrants are sometimes seen on the street, or can be underground.

Hydraulic platform a fire engine with a long, extending arm that can be raised, with a platform on its end.

Jaws of Life® a tool that is used to cut open vehicles if anybody is trapped inside.

Monitor a powerful water cannon, used to spray water over a fire.

Nozzle the part at the end of a hose, where the water or foam comes out.

Pump a device for drawing liquid along a tube.

Retardant a red liquid that slows the progress of a fire.

Resuscitator this is carried and used by an ambulance or fire crew to help revive a casualty.

Siren a device that produces a loud noise to warn people that a rescue vehicle is nearby.

Telescopic ladder a long ladder that folds up into itself.

Turntable ladder some ladders have a turntable at the base to allow them to be turned in a circle.

Tugs these strong boats are used to guide and tow larger boats. They are also used to fight fires.

Index

1926 fire engine

Acknowledgments

Dorling Kindersley would like to thank:
Fleur Star for preparing the index and assisting with the glossary.

Picture credits: